IN GALILEE
and
IN WONDERLAND

THORNTON CHASE

IN GALILEE

by Thornton Chase

and

IN WONDERLAND

by Arthur S. Agnew

KALIMÁT PRESS
LOS ANGELES

Copyright © 1985 by Kalimát Press.

All Rights Reserved.

Manufactured in the United States of America.

Originally published as *In Galilee* and *In Spirit and In Truth* in 1908 by the Bahai Publishing Society. This facsimile reprint is taken from the second edition published in 1921.

Library of Congress Cataloging in Publication Data

Chase, Thornton, 1847-1912.
In Galilee.

Reprint. Originally published: Chicago, Ill., U.S.A.:
Bahai Pub. Society, 1921.
1. Chase, Thornton, 1847-1912. 2. Agnew, Arthur S.
3. Baha'is—Biography. 4. Palestine—Description and travel.
I. Agnew, Arthur S. In wonderland. 1985.
II. Title. III. Title: In wonderland.
BP390.C42 1985   297'.89446   85-9888
ISBN 0-933770-38-3

Cover design by Rick Kjarsgaard

FOREWORD

To visit 'Akká—this was the ardent desire of every early American Bahá'í. Not a few braved the long and difficult journey to that prison-city of the Ottoman Empire, half a world away. They did not speak of meeting with 'Abdu'l-Bahá; their journey was to "attain the presence of the Master." Some 108 persons are officially listed in *The Bahá'í Centenary* as having made the pilgrimage by 1912. Probably there were more. But the vast majority of Western Bahá'ís had not seen 'Abdu'l-Bahá before his historic tour of Europe and America in 1911–1912.

And so, from the time of the first Western pilgrimage sponsored by Phoebe Hearst in 1898–1899, it became the custom for returning pilgrims to recreate their experiences for their fellow believers. Members of the Hearst party returned with recordings of the voices of 'Abdu'l-Bahá and his sister, Bahíyyih Khánum, the Greatest Holy Leaf; they brought back photographs of 'Abdu'l-Bahá and the other members of the Household; they reverently displayed relics related in some way to the person of their Master; they gave numerous talks about their experiences. Several of them also left written accounts of the trip.

Thus began the genre of Bahá'í literature that has come to be known as pilgrim's notes. These consisted, for the most part, of the spoken words of 'Abdu'l-Bahá as they were translated by members of His household and recorded by the visitors. More than twenty were published as booklets during the lifetime of 'Abdu'l-Bahá. Others were published in *Star of the West.* Dozens more were circulated as typed pages. These accounts were used much like scripture in the early American Bahá'í community.

It is not hard to see why—comparing these with the books of the Bible, the scriptures familiar to most of the Western Bahá'ís. Authentic, firsthand accounts of their Master, in the minds of these early believers, must have ranked with the accounts of Christ in the Gospels. Of course, 'Abdu'l-Bahá's station is not equal to that of Christ, but this was by no means clear to all of the early believers: 'Abdu'l-Bahá found Himself repeatedly denying that He was the Return of Christ in His Tablets to America until the end of His life.

Bahá'ís have come to understand that pilgrim's notes cannot be relied upon as sources for the Bahá'í teachings. With the exception of those that have been reviewed and approved by 'Abdu'l-Bahá Himself—and there are notable exceptions, such as *Some Answered Questions*—they do not have the status of Bahá'í scripture. They are of historical interest, but the original motives for their publication are not as compelling today. Nonetheless, for Bahá'ís, such accounts must certainly rank above some biblical chronicles.

There are, however, a few notes from this era which are not only of interest to historians and collectors. These, in addition to giving imperfect records of 'Abdu'l-Bahá's words, also contain accounts of the pilgrims' interactions with Him and describe the day to day activities of His guests. They allow us, to a limited extent, to experience what it was like to stand in the presence of 'Abdu'l-Bahá.

In Galilee by Thornton Chase, and *In Wonderland* by Arthur Agnew, are among a few pilgrim's notes —such as those of Juliet Thompson and May Maxwell—which give well written descriptive accounts of their time in 'Akká. This booklet is also distinguished by the high quality photographs of the Holy Land not found in most similar publications. The two essays were combined under a single cover by the Bahai Publishing Society because they recount the story of the same pilgrimage.

Arthur Agnew's notes of 'Abdu'l-Bahá's words during the visit were published separately under the title *Table Talks at Acca* in 1907. His short appreciation (pp. 75–84) was entitled *In Spirit and In Truth* when the book was first published in 1908. This was changed to *In Wonderland* in the 1921 edition, and the latter title has been retained in this facsimile reprint. This edition reflects the old spellings of Bahá'í terms used before a standard system of transliteration was adopted under Shoghi Effendi.

The believers on pilgrimage with Arthur Agnew and Thornton Chase were: Carl Scheffler; Mary Agnew, Arthur's wife; and their son Ruhullah, named by the Master after the young martyr Varqá. All of the adults were active and prominent members of the Chicago Bahá'í community who had become Bahá'ís through the classes given by Ibrahim Kheiralla in the 1890s. Agnew and Chase had been elected to the Chicago Board of Council, a precursor of the Local Spiritual Assembly, when it was first formed in 1900. Scheffler, only seventeen years old at that time, began his service on the Board a few years later when it was known as the Chicago House of Justice. All three belonged to the group of Bahá'í men who met regularly for lunch at Kimball's, in downtown Chicago, to discuss the Faith.

Thornton Chase, the author of this account, was the most distinguished of the pilgrims. Having declared his belief in Bahá'u'lláh in 1894, he was one of the first four Americans to accept the Faith, and the only one to remain loyal to 'Abdu'l-Bahá after Kheiralla's defection in 1900. For this reason, the Master designated him "the first American believer" and gave him the surname T͟hábit (steadfast).

Chase had been invited to join the Hearst party in 1898, but was unable to get time off from his job at the Union Mutual Life Insurance Company. "I am heart broken," he wrote, "to learn that you are going . . . and it is impossible for me to join you."¹ Unable to be present in person, he asked the others to carry a supplication to 'Abdu'l-Bahá so that he might receive a written reply especially for himself. This request was granted. Early in the following year, Chase became one of the first American Bahá'ís to receive a Tablet from 'Abdu'l-Bahá.

It was not until 1907—nearly nine years later—that Chase found it possible to make the journey to the Holy Land. It was not a good season for pilgrimage. The schemings of Covenant-breakers had recently resulted in greater restrictions on 'Abdu'l-Bahá, and the presence of Western disciples was always a danger to Him. Earlier in 1907, some American Bahá'ís had gotten as far as Haifa, only to learn that conditions made it impossible for them to visit the Master in 'Akká. Chase's party was allowed to cross the bay to 'Akká, but their visit was cut short unexpectedly when the governor in Beirut was notified by telegram of their arrival.

Chase was devastated by this misfortune. His companion, Carl Scheffler, recalled:

> Mr. Chase was so moved by this departure that he spoke no word during the entire journey and not until he again entered the hospice of the Little Child in Haifa were his tears dried.²

He was only reconciled to this sudden separation by 'Abdu'l-Bahá's promise that he would see Him again in the near future. This second meeting, however, was to take place on another plane. In 1912, Chase's untimely death prevented him from seeing the Master during His visit to America. In October of that year, 'Abdu'l-Bahá traveled to Los Angeles specifically for the purpose of making a pilgrimage to the grave of Thornton Chase, where he extolled him in the highest terms.

Chase spent only four days with 'Abdu'l-Bahá in 'Akká. And during this time, as he recalled, "the opportunity did not appear for any more than a few minutes privately with our Lord."[3] The pilgrims saw Him mostly at mealtimes. The rest of the time was spent with other members of the Household. Their names are found here as frequently as that of the Master: Mírzá Asadu'lláh, whom Chase had met when he came to Chicago, Ḥájí Mírzá Ḥaydar-'Alí, the famous Bahá'í teacher; Mírzá Muḥammad-Qulí, the faithful half brother of Bahá'u'lláh; Mírzá Munír and Mírzá Núru'd-Dín, sons of the famous Bahá'í scribe Zaynu'l-Muqarrabín. There was also Shoghi Effendi, then a boy, the future Guardian of the Bahá'í Faith. If 'Abdu'l-Bahá was not always present, His overpowering spirit can nonetheless be sensed throughout the narrative.

More important, after all, than the amount of time a pilgrim spent with the Master was the quality of that time—a matter conditioned on spiritual capacity. Some had stayed for weeks, even months, in 'Abdu'l-Bahá's house, but few were attracted to Him as Thornton Chase was. "How the heart responds to the least word from that

Center of the Covenant," he wrote.[4] Of Chase, Scheffler recalls:

> In the presence of the Master he seemed completely melted and overcome by the love of 'Abdu'l-Bahá, and the love and kindness of the believers. Not all the experiences in that Holy Household were purely pleasurable, for 'Abdu'l-Bahá in his kindly manner corrected many concepts that, in spite of a broad vision and deep understanding, still were wrong. That 'Abdu'l-Bahá loved him dearly was obvious, and his response was that of a loving and trusting son.[5]

The Master Himself recalled that during his short stay in 'Akká, Chase "became free from the troubles of this world."[6]

For this Bahá'í, only a few hours in the presence of the Master had to suffice. They did. His short visit inspired him to dedicate the remaining years of his life to the service of the Bahá'í Cause. It is hoped that the reprint of this account of those precious moments may do the same for a new generation of believers.

RICHARD HOLLINGER
LOS ANGELES
MARCH 1985

NOTES

1. Thornton Chase to Ibrahim Kheiralla, September 19, 1898, in private hands.
2. Carl Scheffler, "Thornton Chase: The First American Bahá'í," *World Order,* vol. 11, no. 5 (August 1945) p. 157.
3. Thornton Chase to Charles M. Remey, January 19, 1910, Thornton Chase papers, National Bahá'í Archives, Wilmette, Ill.
4. Thornton Chase to Ella Cooper, November 14, 1908, Ella Cooper papers, San Francisco Bahá'í Archives.
5. Scheffler, "Thornton Chase," p. 156.
6. "Abdul-Baha at the Grave of Thornton Chase," *Star of the West,* vol. 3, no. 13 (November 4, 1912) p. 14.

In Galilee

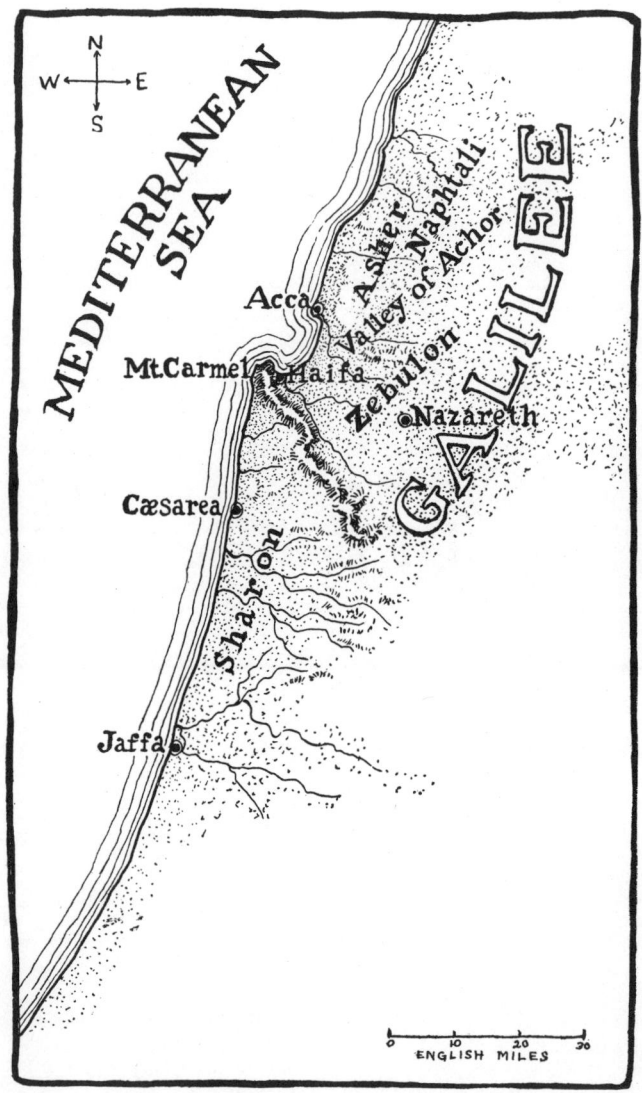

"Nevertheless the dimness shall not be such as was in her vexation, when at the first he lightly afflicted the land of Zebulon and the land of Naphtali and afterward did more grievously afflict her by the <u>way of the sea,</u> beyond Jordan, in Galilee of the nations.

"The people that walked in darkness have seen a great light: they that dwell in the land of the shadow of death, upon them hath the light shined."

Isaiah 9:1, 2.

"The wilderness and the solitary place shall be glad for them; and the desert shall rejoice, and blossom as the rose.

"It shall blossom abundantly, and rejoice even with joy and singing: the glory of Lebanon shall be given unto it, the excellency of Carmel and Sharon, they shall see the <u>glory of the Lord</u> and the excellency of our God."

"And an highway shall be there, and a way, and it shall be called The way of holiness."

Isaiah 35:1, 2, 8.

"Out of Asher his bread shall be fat, and he shall yield royal dainties."

Gen. 49:20.

"And Sharon shall be a fold of flocks, and the valley of Achor a place for the herds to lie down in, for my people that have sought me."

Isaiah 65:10.

"And I will give her her vineyards from thence and the Valley of Achor for a <u>door of hope:</u> and she shall sing there as in the days of her youth, as in the day when she came up out of the land of Egypt."

Hosea 2:15.

Jaffa

On April 8th, 1907, a bright, cool day, our little party, Mr. Agnew with wife and boy, Mr. Scheffler and I, gathered on the deck of the Khedivial steamer "Assuan," lying off the ancient port of Jaffa in Syria. Around us were other Americans, tourists, teachers, and missionaries bound for Haifa and some for Beirut about 70 miles north from Haifa, where a Presbyterian college is located. There were also Turkish officers and Egyptian Beys, the latter in European dress with red fezzes, and a number of Franciscan monks with close cropped heads, dressed in the typical brown hooded robes and sandals. On the lower deck, where they had slept rolled up in blankets through the night, were the steerage passengers, crowded groups of Arab and Turkish men, women and children in native costumes.

After noon we left our anchorage and sailed northward, over the blue Mediterranean, from Jaffa toward Carmel, skirting the broken, rocky edge of the Syrian Coast with its background of green slopes and distant hills. Our hearts were so affected with thankfulness to God and with the beauty and import of that Land of Promise that we spoke but little to each other and in subdued tones. Our tongues were bound in golden silence, our eyes searched the ancient scenes and looked keenly to the north for the first glimpse of Mount Carmel and Acca and we longed for the approaching goal of our pilgrimage. Gradually the bold front of the mountain swelled up from the coastline, and a little after, when the lowering sun slanted its brightness across the waters, the while walls of the little fortress of Acca rose from the ocean and gleamed afar like a marble island in a turquoise sea. You can be sure that our eyes looked long and steadily at the little cluster of white as we came nearer and nearer to that "Door of Hope." Haifa was not to be seen, as it nestles within the elbow of Carmel on its northern side, until the ship had passed by the mountain and turned inward toward the town.

We arrived off Haifa at 5 P. M. As the steamer anchored, a fleet of boats came racing toward the ship. They represented different landing Companies, the Hamburg-American, Clark's, Cook's, etc. Each was manned by eight to ten swarthy, sturdy, red-fezzed boatmen handling as many long, heavy, square-handled oars. The race was in earnest, all eager for passengers and backsheesh. As they came nearer, at a signal from the leader of the crew, each rower placed one bare foot on the cross seat before him, leaped up as high as he could, pulled back his oar with a long, powerful sweep, sinking down to his seat, and then sprang up again for another mighty pull, accompanying each effort with a quick, strong call of encouragement: "Haley! Haley! Haley! Haaa! Saleh!" It was an exciting welcome, the crews rising and sinking, the boats lifting through the waves and almost in collision, the stirring cries keeping time and becoming louder and more intense as they approached.

"Cook's" arrived first and took our party to the landing place. When entering the boat the passenger has to submit entirely to the crew. One goes down the slippery steps on the ship's side to the little hanging platform and as the light boat rises on a wave to meet it, one or two of the Arab sailors seizes him (or her) in his arms, holds him as the boat sinks and bears him to a seat. The process is repeated at the landing place where each person is lifted by strong arms from the boat as it rises to the dock. So we entered Palestine.

THE WAY OF THE SEA—HAIFA TO ACCA

A crowd of people was on the pier and as we went up toward the street, a familiar face appeared and one of us exclaimed: "There's Mirza Assadu'llah!" As we hurried to Cook's carriage I managed to touch his hand in passing and received a pressure of recognition, but no further attention.

HAIFA.

We were taken to the Catholic "Hospice of the Little Child," conducted by German Sisters, where we had spacious rooms, plainly furnished and scrupulously clean. Over the door of each room was an inscription dedicating it to one of the Saints. Mr. Scheffler and I had the room of "St. John." In it were two neat beds, plain chairs, washbowls, and matting on the stone floors. In the dining room all the guests sat at one long table. The food was plain and wholesome. Mirza Assadu-llah, with Mirza Mohsin and Mirza Jallal, called in the evening and we were happy to meet them. Others were in the reception room who understood both English and Arabic and they were listening intently, curious to learn what acquaintance or business the Americans had with the Persians. They would not have understood that only the love of our hearts drew us together. We learned that word of our arrival would be sent the following day and arrangements made for going to Acca as soon as convenient. We were rejoiced that we should soon enter the presence of the renowned teacher whom we love to call "The Master." He, however, asks us not to so call him, as he says the titles "Master" and "Lord" belonged to Jesus and he wishes to be called by his proper and perfect title—Abdul-Baha, the Servant of God. He asks each one of the friends to *first learn this station of his clearly,* that he may know *in his heart* the meaning of Abdul-Baha!

We slept well that first night in Syria. In the morning we went up the hill to Mirza Assad-u'llah's home, passing through the German Colony. This Colony was established in Haifa in 1843 in expectation of the second coming of Christ, which they claimed was prophesied to occur soon after that time on Mount Carmel. Over the doors of school and church and of many houses are inscriptions signifying their expectation, such as "Der Herr ist Nahe" (The Lord is near), etc. Yet they know not that the prophecy has been fulfilled and that the Lord has indeed been at their very doors.

A HAIFA HOME

Mirza Assadu'llah and Mirza Mohsin welcomed us warmly. They inquired after the friends in America, naming many of them. They asked concerning the growth and condition of the great Cause and rejoiced at any news of love and unity in service among the friends. Mirza Mohsin interpreted.

THE HOLY LAND.

The view was fine of the city below and of the Tomb of the Bab high up on the mountain side above. We could scarcely appreciate the sacredness of that historic ground, but as we looked up to the Tomb and thought of its meaning, of the wonderful lives of the Bab and of Baha'o'llah, of their sufferings and apparent defeat at the hands of oppressors, and of the victories which are now following the Word of Truth for which they suffered, we began to realize that we had indeed entered the border of the "Holy Land," the land that Abraham knew, where Melchizedek dwelt, where Elijah prophesied and sacrificed on Carmel unto the Lord whose fire descended upon his altar and put to shame the hosts of Baal. It was on the top of Carmel that Elijah bowed himself down upon the earth and put his face between his knees before the Lord, and there, "at the seventh time,"
 . . . "Behold, there ariseth a cloud out of the sea, as small as a man's hand." "And it came to pass in a little while, that the heaven grew black with clouds and wind, and there was a

great rain." How prophetic becomes this history in the light of present events!

There Jesus walked and taught. Capernaum is near, Nazareth twelve miles away and it is but a short distance to the Sea of Galilee where the fishers drew their nets and left them at the command—"Come! Follow me! and I will make you fishers of men." This was the land of Zebulun and Naphtali, by the way of the sea, which was covered with darkness until that Light shone forth upon it. And now again it is plunged in gross darkness, all heedless of the Light which has again arisen upon it, of the Glory that is within it, which is even now flaming forth from its ancient prison to the farthest bounds of mankind, the Light which is "the same yesterday, today and forever" and which shall illumine the darkness of ignorance and awaken man to the Dawning Day of Service, Love and Peace.

The afternoon following our arrival in Haifa, I was writing at a table on the little veranda of the Hospice, looking toward Acca nine miles away, when a beautiful thing appeared. The day had been showery and about four o'clock a splendid double rainbow shone forth. It seemed to rest on the eastern part of Haifa where the gate opens out to the "Way of the Sea"; its further end was directly at the gate of Acca and the western sun shone brightly on the glistening city just beyond. The long, inward curving shore line of the blue sea with its white breakers swept in under the rainbow, and beneath its glorious arch the distant Lebanon hills showed their purple sides and snow capped ranges. For over half an hour that vision of beauty remained. PEACE! There was its sign, declared of old. There was the ancient symbol of the creative Holy Spirit brooding over that Place of Promise, and I seemed to see beneath its arc of glory temples of silver with domes of gold, gates of pearl and all precious stones, and I realized that —"The city hath no need of the sun, neither of the moon, to shine upon it, for the glory of God did lighten it, and the lamp thereof is the Lamb."

"And he said unto me, Son of Man, this is the place of my throne, and the place of the soles of my feet, where I will dwell in the midst of the children of Israel forever." "And the name of the city from that day shall be, The Lord is there."

MOUNT CARMEL.

The next day, according to arrangement, Mr. and Mrs. Agnew went to Acca while Mr. Scheffler and I moved to the Hotel Pross on the top of Mount Carmel, where we were met by Mr. Snyder, a German minister and missionary who keeps it. We found him a kindly host, quiet and simple. Everything was thoroughly clean and comfortable. Several English and American women tourists were there, school teachers, and some missionaries returning from India. They were resting before going to Nazareth, Damascus and Beirut.

In the evening a lady told of her trip that day to Acca. She said the house of "The New Prophet" was pointed out and some one suggested that she might like to meet him. She assented, and one went into his garden and asked permission for the meeting, which was granted. He was a man of striking and attractive appearance and met her most graciously and presented her with a rose he was carrying. Through an interpreter she asked him several questions, which he answered in a courteous and gentle manner, and she could see no difference in what he said from the teachings of Jesus.

Considerable conversation ensued and one lady said she had heard that Americans sometimes came all the way there expressly to visit him and receive his teachings and she wondered how they could be such fools. She also supposed they brought much money to him. Mr. Scheffler and I sat there longing to open our mouths and loosen our tongues, but beyond asking some simple questions, we remained silent. One asked the lady what she had done with the rose. She replied that she had pressed it and intended to keep it as a souvenir.

In the afternoon we wandered over to the headland that rises boldly from the sea. Roadsides and fields were painted with blossoms, and we delighted in their variety, colors and

A SQUARE OF BROWNISH YELLOW LIMESTONE

fragrance. There were myriads of flowers, daisies, forget-me-nots, sweet peas, lilies, roses, and the flaming red poppies everywhere. We gathered them as we went, only to drop some as we found others more beautiful. We were happy as children, wandering over the hills and talking of things most dear to our hearts. When we returned to the hotel we filled every available dish with flowers and pressed what we could in our diaries.

THE TOMB OF THE BAB.

The next day we walked to the Tomb of the Bab. We went on the smooth, broad road along the ridge until we came to the top of the trail which goes almost directly down the side, the same on which we had seen donkeys loaded with wood picking their way the day before. It was very steep and all of loose, crumbling stones.

The sides of the mountain are terraced and cultivated everywhere. The larger loose stones are gathered into walls; the rich reddish brown soil and smaller stones are leveled or gently sloped from the foot of one wall to the top of another, thus making steps from ten to twenty or thirty feet wide, in which are fig and olive trees, grapes and vegetables. Men and women were loosening the soil with mattocks.

After going down about 1,000 feet we came to the road and found a neat carriage way between walls leading from the main roadway to the tomb. It is a square of brownish yellow limestone with white iron paneled doors, simple in architecture and with little outside ornament. A considerable space was cut out from the side of the mountain and leveled around the tomb. A portion of it is a stone surface in which is the mouth of a large cistern for water. Another portion is a flower garden, beyond which is the house of the caretaker, a Persian

TRAIL DOWN MT. CARMEL

ANOTHER VIEW OF THE TOMB

Bahai. He lives there with his wife and baby and has an Arab assistant.

When we came onto the stone platform we saw no one, but in a few minutes the Arab appeared, came over to us and said "Acca" and "Abbas Effendi." We smiled and nodded assent. He went to the garden and brought a flower to each of us. Then the caretaker, Rahmatu'llah, came from the house with his little baby boy and greeted us. He brought out chairs and I asked him to sit with the baby for a picture. He excused himself, went into the house and after a few minutes appeared dressed in his best clothes, a long, black coat hiding the flowing costume in which I wished to photograph him. But the picture was never taken, for just then two Persians appeared, who had come up the trail from below. They greeted him joyfully with the "Greatest Name," embracing him, and then, as we also repeated that Name, they took us in their arms with expressions of great gladness and praises to God.

They were M. Mohammed Ali Yazdi and Hadji Mohammed Schushtari of Cairo with his seven year old boy. They could speak no English, but they had a message for us which was that "Cooks" would come for us the next morning to take us to Acca. Although we understood their meaning, it was further assured by the Persian who went into the house to consult his wife, who must have known some English, for he returned saying—"Tomorrow morning, go Acca."

Then the door of the tomb was opened and we were invited to enter. It is simple and beautiful, although it is not finished. It is divided into three large compartments, a center and two sides, and these into sections named after notable Babis and Bahais. The floor of the center is slightly raised. The roof is in arches, those of the sides being at right angles to the arches of the center. We bowed in silence for a few minutes, then withdrew and bade our friends adieu, while they exclaimed again and again—"Koosh amadeed! Koosh amadeed!"—the Persian expression for "You are welcome!" As we left the road and began to climb the trail we looked back and saw them going into the little grove of ten cypress trees in a circle on the hillside just above the tomb. It is said that Baha'o'llah used often to sit in that grove which commands a beautiful view of the sea and the Valley of Acca.

When we had gone up the trail some distance and reached the end of our first breath, we rested and noticed a lithe young Arab hurrying up from below. When he reached us we found that he had a note from Cook's, saying that they would call for us the next morning, at any hour we would name, to take us to Acca. The messenger was on his way to the hotel and finding us on the way saved him a long climb but lost him no backsheesh. Then we hastened up the mountain with joy in our hearts and out feet lightened by the glad anticipations for the next day.

THE WAY OF THE SEA.

April 12th greeted us with a beautiful morning. The great day had arrived, the day for which we had looked and longed. We were really going to Acca. We started at 7 o'clock in the open carriage with three horses abreast. That ride on the good, hard road along the mountain crest, then down the rocky sides, by walled terraces, farms and groves, was a delight. We understood some of the reasons why Carmel was called the Mountain of Beauty. We breathed the sweet air and watched the play of color in sunlight and shadow as floating clouds moved over the long slopes and rolling hills. Snow turbaned Hermon and the encircling purple robed steeps of Lebanon stood in silent guard over the valleys beneath. Each wind and turn of the road changed the view. Far below the azure sea glistened, and long, white rolls of surf chased one another up the sandy beach. In hazy distance a faint cluster of white marked the walls of the city of our desire. All else was but the setting for that gem of divine choosing, for it is the "Chosen Land."

We stopped a few minutes at Cook's, then drove down through Haifa, halting a little at Mirza Hadi's store, then through the market square to the eastern gate, a narrow curved archway in the wall, and out onto the beach. After a little we came near to a drove of camels that were being loaded with rough blocks of building stone where they had camped the night before, and there Mirza Assadu'llah joined us.

Then began the nine mile drive along the beautiful curve of the Mediterranean shore, most of the way in the water where the sand is hard and the surf plays "tag" with the carriage wheels, while the horse hoofs clatter and splash a quick tattoo through the gliding water. Higher up the beach are mounds of loose sand

LOADED WITH BUILDING STONE

THE APPROACH TO ACCA

with long, wiry bunch grasses and occasional tall date palms. When we crossed the two rivers that run into the sea, we rode out forty or fifty yards from the shore so as to follow the sand bars formed by the breakers as they meet the outflowing rivers. Sometimes the water was up to the box of the carriage and the horses had to strain to pull us through. We passed carriages coming from Acca, pack-trains of asses and camels, flocks of little, black, lop-eared goats, foot travelers, fishing boats and fishermen standing far out in the surf, casting their round nets as their fathers have done for decades of centuries. Ever before us was the walled city, rising clearer and larger from the water by which it is nearly surrounded.

It is ancient beyond the knowledge of man, perhaps the oldest city in the world. Its depths have not been explored, but ruin has followed ruin, and city after city, none knows how many, has been built on the remains of the past. It has ever been a point of vantage and of strife and is renowned for its desperate sieges and defences.

There are still remnants of the ruins of Alexander ("Balas"), king of Syria 150 years before Christ. The Genoese captured it in 1104 and Saladin drove them out in 1187, only to be overcome by the last victorious assault of the Christian Crusaders under Cœur de Lion in 1191. There Napoleon was brought to bay in 1799 and forced to abandon his dream of Oriental conquest by that "grain of sand" as he called it. It was taken by storm in 1832 by Ibrahim Pasha, who in turn was overthrown by the British, Austrian and Turkish allies in 1840. It has witnessed many scenes of war and siege, of hunger and thirst, of torture and death. Still do the soldiers patrol its walls, it may be destined yet again to bear the shock of battle. It is a tomb of warriors, a whited sepulchre full within of dead men's bones, but from that tomb shall arise in this millennial dawn the Spirit of Peace, going forth to a glorious victory over the hearts of men.

How wonderful is the work of God! The seed must needs be buried in the dark dungeon of earth before it can bring forth the living tree; the Word must be hidden in the crypts of death, in the tomb of lowliness and rejection, surrounded by the darkness of ignorance and clay of prejudice ere it can send forth the Truth that makes men free, the Light that illumines their souls, the Love that ripens the fruits of righteousness, holiness and beauty in the Kingdom of God.

THE PRISON CITY.

When within a half mile of the city lying on the point of land out in the sea, we left the beach and entered a roadway between fine shade trees, leading to the gate in the wall. We passed through the gate into a market place filled with men and animals, and through the inner gate curving under the second wall, and so into the prison city. Mirza Assadu'llah had left us, and we went on with Cook's driver as tourists do who visit Acca; yet we were probably recognized as Americans and as we entered the city we were greeted with a shower of stones which rattled harmlessly against the carriage. Possibly they were thrown in a spirit of mischief. A rabble of youths and boys ran after us all the way across the city to the entrance of the house of Abdul-Baha. There the driver got down from his seat and drove them away. Our progress had been slow as the three horses filled the ways and crowded the people against the walls, and the turns in the alley like streets were sharp and narrow and made with difficulty.

We did not know we had reached our destination until we saw a Persian gentleman, and then another and another, step out at the entrance and smile at us. We alighted and they conducted us through the arched, red brick entrance to an open court, across it to a long flight of stone steps, broken and ancient, leading to the highest story and into a small walled court open to the

GARDEN AND TENT OF ABDUL-BAHA

sky, where was the upper chamber assigned to us, which adjoined the room of Abdul-Baha. The buildings are all of stone, whitewashed and plastered, and it bears the aspect of a prison.

Our windows looked out over the garden and tent of Abdul-Baha on the sea side of the house. That garden is bounded on one side by the house of the Governor, which overlooks it, and on another by the inner wall of fortification. A few feet beyond that is the outer wall upon the sea, and between these two are the guns and soldiers constantly on guard. A sentry house stands at one corner of the wall and garden, from which the sentry can see the grounds and the tent where

RECEPTION ROOM OF ABDUL-BAHA

Abdul-Baha meets transient visitors and the officials who often call on him. Thus all his acts outside of the house itself are visible to the Governor from his windows and to the men on guard. Perhaps that is one reason why the officials so often become his friends. No one, with humanity, justice, or mercy in his heart, could watch Abdul-Baha long without admiring and loving him for the beautiful qualities constantly displayed.

Five days we remained within those walls, prisoners with Him who dwells in that "Greatest Prison." It is a prison of peace, of love and service. No wish, no desire is there save the good of mankind, the peace of the world, the acknowledgment of the Fatherhood of God and the mutual rights of men as His creatures, His children. Indeed, the real prison, the suffocating atmosphere, the separation from all true heart desires, the bond of world conditions, is outside of those stone walls, while within them is the freedom and pure aura of the Spirit of God. All troubles, tumults, worries or anxieties for worldly things are barred out there.

Over the head of each one of the exiles in that prison hangs constantly the sword of Damocles, suspended by a hair, and the coming of any American or English pilgrim sets that hair to vibrating. This is not because of enmity from the Government, which shows a just and generous spirit, but because the enemies to the Cause of God are always trying to incite troubles and suspicions. While we were there a message was sent to the Government, by certain of the opposers, complaining of our coming and stay and trying to falsely attach political significance to it; therefore it was deemed best that we should leave. After that, further efforts were made to bring troubles upon the friends. This illustrates the volcanic condition there and the serious causes, ever present, for mortal fears and anxieties; yet there is the abode of peace, happiness, content, assurance and supreme faith. Even were that awful sword to fall and sever the Head from the body, faith would only be strengthened and service be multiplied, so perfect is the assurance and certainty that this is the Work of God, destined to victory over the heart of mankind, and the accomplishment of the peaceful Kingdom of God in the spirits of men over the whole world.

While there and now I realize the meaning of Mr. Winterburn's expression that—"The world seemed miles and centuries away." Worldly matters indeed press with keen intrusion on that family and those sweet friends in the prison of Acca, and they cause anxieties, too, sometimes, but so mighty there is the Spirit of God, so absorbing are the considerations of spiritual things, so uplifting those considerations, so overwhelming is the ocean of the Word, that all other matters slink away, out of sight, and Man stands erect in the bracing air of the Spirit with its life-giving strength.

In a Tablet He has said: "Set all desires aside, leave worldly matters, devote thyself to God, be filled with the Spirit, guide the people to safety, and perfume the nostrils with the holy fragrances which emanate from the Kingdom of EL-ABHA."

"By the life of Baha! He who is filled with the love of Baha and forgets all things, the Holy Spirit will be heard from his lips, and the Spirit of Life will fill his heart, the lights of the Sign will shine forth from his face, and words will issue from his mouth in strands of pearls, and all sickness and disease will be healed by the laying on of his hands."

THE WELCOME.

Mirza Moneer and Mirza Noure-Din (sons of the famous and learned Jenabi Zain), and

Mirza Hussein Afnan, a student at the Beirut college, all English speakers, were with us during the few minutes until the arrival of Abdul-Baha. Some one said, "The Master!"—and he came into the room with a free, striding step, welcomed us in a clear, ringing voice—"Mahrhabba! Mahrhabba!" (Welcome! Welcome!)— and embraced us with kisses as would a father his son, or as would brothers after a long absence. It is no wonder that some have thought that the Master loved them more than all others, because he hesitates not to express his love and he truly *loves all humanity in each one.* He is the great Humanitarian and each friend is to him the representative of all mankind.

He bade us be seated on the little divan; he sat on the high, narrow bed at one side of the room, drew up one foot under him, asked after our health, our trip, bade us be happy, and expressed his happiness that we had safely arrived. Then, after a few minutes, he again grasped our hands and abruptly left us. The friends also went out and left us alone. We looked at each other. I think we had not spoken at all except to answer "yes" or "no." We could not. We knew not what to say. But our hearts were full of joyful tears, because we were "at home." His welcoming spirit banished strangeness, as though we had always known him. It was as if, after long journeyings, weariness, trials and searchings, we had at last reached home. The world of wanderings was left at the outer gate, we had entered into peace, joy, love, home. Those were moments of deep happiness; yet I could not fully realize the great blessedness or that meeting, which was the goal of my hope; but now its remembrance has become my joy and the treasure of my heart. I was filled with wonder at his simplicity, with admiration for his strength and dignity and love for his tenderness; these, mingled with delight and thankfulness, possessed me.

ABDUL-BAHA.

I have been asked to describe Abdul-Baha, but hesitate to do so. It is not his personality that he wishes the friends to consider. Yet so many long to know even a little of the appearance of this one whom they love, not having seen, that I will try to tell of him as he appeared to me. I saw a strikingly handsome man, tall and kingly. He wore a white fez with the small turban-kerchief wound around. This, the symbol of wisdom and learning among Mohammedans, was the only outward insignia of his station. A long, dark coat or cloak was worn over a dove colored undercoat. He is not thin or anaemic, but has the appearance of strong health. Although of medium height he is commanding in appearance and I can never think of him as less than six feet tall. His bright, fair face, light brown in complexion, was framed in silvery white beard and moustache. Usually his hair, or much of it, was tucked up under the fez. His nose was large, straight and strong. The mouth was rather full and very gentle. Deep under the broad forehead, and shaded by white, thick eyebrows, shone the wondrous eyes, large, prominent, brilliant, penetrating and kind. Around the dark pupil and brown iris is that wonderful blue circle which sometimes makes the eyes look a perfect blue. Any description of them is only an attempt, no more. In repose the face expressed a dignity, intelligence and nobility which none would dare to disrespect. Conscious power and authority were there enthroned. He assumed nothing; his powers were natural, his sincerity thorough, his affection pure. His smile charmed and attracted friends to him.

He had the stride and freedom of a king—or shepherd. My impression of him was that of a lion, a kingly, masterful Man of the most sweet and generous disposition. I had formed an idea of Jesus as very meek, humble, lowly, gentle, quiet, soft and sweet, and I looked for such another one. I have revised my idea of Jesus and now, as I read his Words, I see in that one of the past a Man of Authority, whose words were clear and forceful, penetrating the hearts as with a two-edged sword. I found in Abdul-Baha a man, strong, powerful, without a thought as to any act, as free and unstilted as a father with his family or a boy with playmates. Yet each movement, his walk, his greeting, his sitting down and rising up were eloquent of power, full of dignity, freedom and ability.

In his presence all are small and they are conscious of this. They show a deference to him that could not be excelled before the most absolute monarch, hesitating to approach him unbidden, humbly bowing when he passes, and halting afar off when coming into his presence. This was not of his doing or will, but purely from their recognition of the Spiritual Power proceeding from him and through their intense love and respect for him. He seemed utterly unconscious of their deference. He extends love to every one; he draws near to them; he invites them; he loves to serve them, even in little things. He demands no awe, no reverence, no separation, but is an elder Brother of affection and sweetness. He is gentle but not weak; sweet and powerful; humble and mighty; no bar or restraint is there, but winsome love and attraction. His work accomplished daily is very great, and yet much time is given to social and official affairs. He is abrupt in manner, the abruptness of power, but most courteous and charming. There is no aloofness in him; he invites all to be prisoners of love and fellow-servers of humanity with him. He spoke in brief, pithy expressions, intoned in medium pitch with a clear vibrant voice. No words were wasted. He said:

"The Bounty of God is flowing. The Power of the Kingdom of God will overcome all. It will not be long before the great result will appear." "The Blessed Beauty has put in our hands the lamp of teachings. By this Light the world will be illumined." "America will be enlightened very much, and from there light will be sent to other places." "I hope that the East and the West will become one, also the North and the South, and that all differences shall be removed." "The Power of the Word of God will accomplish this."

THE MID-DAY MEAL.

Within an hour we were called to the noon meal. The Master again welcomed us and motioned each to his seat at the table. There were twelve—Abdul-Baha, Mirza Mohammed Gholi (the beautiful brother of Baha'o'llah Mirza Mohsin (son-in-law of Abdul-Baha), Mirza Assadu'llah, Mizra Moneer and Mirza Noured-Din (interpreters), Shogi Afnan (grandson of the Master), Mr. Agnew, wife and son, Mr. Scheffler and this servant. All stood in respect until the Host sat. Food was first offered him, but he refused until all were served when he took some also. Then looking around the table and noting that none were eating, he said: 'Bismillah!" (In the Name of God), signifying that we should eat. That one expression, accompanied with his brilliant smile, was a blessing.

After the first course was ended and the plates removed, he spoke of our meeting there together in affection, joy and harmony, saying that it was by the power of the Word of God. There

CRUMBLING ROCK ON MT. CARMEL

might be other meetings of people from different parts of the earth, but they were not like this where we were drawn together by the fires of love in our hearts. Then he talked of the necessity of decomposition of all things before a recomposition could take place, and said that it was the power of the Word of God which decomposed the self of man in order that he might be recreated.

Mr. Scheffler and I looked at each other, because, that very morning, while riding down Mt. Carmel nine miles away, we had noted the crumbling rock and rich soil, and had spoken the thought that came to us—that the rock had to be tested, disintegrated and decomposed into soil before its chemical values could be released and transmuted into the higher kingdom of plant life. And there, at noon of the same day, Abdul-Baha brought forth the same subject and gave us his beautiful instructions upon it. It has been often remarked that he answers the thoughts of the friends before they are expressed to him.

Another course of delicious Persian food was served by Bashi, the young East Indian from Bombay who came and offered his life as a servant in that household, and then again Abdul-Baha uttered words of wisdom and instruction. Then came the dessert, and, after a few words more, he arose, and all arose and stood in respectful deference as he left us to go to his tent in the garden to supply other souls with the food of their need.

This meal's experience was repeated daily, sometimes twice, at noon and evening. From our room window we often saw him walking in the garden, meeting people, and when he could get away for a few minutes from other cares, he would come up to our room and talk with us. Each conversation started with some simple reference to a natural thing, the weather, food, a stone, tree, water, the prison, a garden or a bird, our coming, or some little act of service, and this base would be woven into a parable and teaching of wisdom and simplicity, showing the oneness of all Spiritual Truth, and adapting it always to *the life,* both of the individual and of mankind. All of his words are directed toward *helping men to live.* Unless questions of metaphysics, dogmas and doctrines be introduced, he seldom mentions them. He speaks easily, clearly, in brief phrases, each of which is a gem. Whatever the lesson may be it always culminates in some teaching of unity, for the whole purpose of this greatest Revelation is Unity, the teaching of the Oneness of God, the oneness of His Manifestors, the oneness of man, the oneness of the universe; and all this oneness is the expression of love. It is love manifest, love that unites, binds all together, that permeates all existence and draws it into oneness with its Creator who is love itself.

O son of man!
"My oneness is my design. I have designed it for thee; therefore clothe thyself with it. Thus thou mayest be a star of my omnipresence forever." H. W. 65

UNIVERSAL LOVE.

All difference, all lack of harmony, all disunity in the universe is due to lack of love, or to changing universal love into individual love, putting self-interest in the place of the welfare of the whole. But in Abdul-Baha is never a trace of self-interest. Each thought, each word of his is for the universal love, the divinity of man in his oneness with mankind. He speaks not from the self, but from the Spirit; yet his speech is that of the man, simple, direct, as of a father to his son. "Are you well?" "Are you happy?" This would be an oft repeated greeting. "You have come in a good time." "Since you have come the weather has been beautiful." Such simple remarks as these would prelude an instructive discourse of ten or fifteen minutes, or possibly three or four minutes. We took no note of time.

About half past nine in the evening he came to Mr. Agnew's room where we were gathered. He was very tired, and, after greeting us, he sat on the divan and called Mr. Scheffler and this servant to sit on either side. He took our hands and for fifteen minutes or more he held them in his, often grasping them with a rapid, strong, vibrating grip while he talked. He said he had been sorely tried that day by strangers, but that for the sake of love he had been most kind to them, as we must ever be, showing the greatest kindness to those who opposed. He said he was now happy in the company of friends, and then he talked again of decomposition and composition, showing that one accompanied disunion, disagreement and separation and caused death, but the other brought unification and life. Then abruptly he arose and left us, going to his room, and we also retired for our first night's sleep in the prison city of Acca, in that house where had lived the Great Manifestation of God, the Blessed Perfection, Baha'o'llah, with saints and martyrs in the holy Cause. In the adjoining room rested the Servant of God, Abdul-Baha, the faithful, patient Establisher of the New Kingdom of Heaven in the hearts of men. For a while we listened to the sentry on duty at the guarded wall by the sea, chanting his sacred supplications in darkness—and then we slept.

DAWN IN ACCA.

It seemed not an hour when I was awakened by a clear, high voice proclaiming between the earth and heaven the Oneness of God, chanting the Koran from the high balcony of the nearby minaret. The long, sweet, quivering tones rang through the silent air, invoking worship from the faithful. The bell-like notes invited the dawn, the first ray of which may have been visible from the tower height as it heralded the victory of light over the dark and sleeping world.

Soon a voice farther away declared another watchman calling the sleepers to awake and greet the morn. The sweet, vibrant chants continued until day looked in at our window, and the birds chirped and fluttered around the open court, singing their songs of welcome to the light. We, too, with joyful hearts praised God for His great Light of Revelation and Truth.

What wonder that the Moslem cannot be swerved from his worship and loyalty to the One God and to His great prophet Mohammed. His first, baby lispings were praises and affirmations of Him from the sacred Koran; his first consciousness in every day of his life is the voice of man proclaiming: "There is no God but God, and Mohammed is His Prophet!" That holy, basic principle is inculcated "Line upon line, precept upon precept" at each awakening from sleep, at each beginning of active life, and declared five times in each day from his cradle to his grave. It becomes a part of him; from its established throne in his brain it repels all suggestion of a triune God, and makes his life, whatever it may be in other respects, a fortress against unfaith.

It was Sunday, and soon the jangle of chimes sounded from the Syrian Church, calling the Christians to early Mass. The morning was beautiful, fresh and still, and the tones of opposing mosque and church sounded only of peace. Alas, that religion should ever bring aught else between God's children! But the military cornet's call told us of the fortified city and of the soldier ready for attack or defense for the greed of man and "in the Name of God." Across the garden the blue sea sparkled with little ripples and washed the base of the rampart wall a few yards away. An old, rusty cannon lay on the rock in the corner bastion, telling of war long past, and the guard with his musket walked by the narrow gateway between the corner and the court. In the distance the dark blue mound of Carmel was crowned with rosy mists. All nature spoke of peace, and only man of strife.

At 7 o'clock I saw M. Assadu'llah Kishani sweeping the rough and broken stone flight of outside steps as carefully as though they were of alabaster; another of the friends was dipping from the well and watering the plants of the garden, and others were attending to the needs of the kitchen. The care, earnestness and pleasure with which these things were done showed the spirit of love in the service. Indeed, it is evident there that service is esteemed a privilege and is a cause of happiness. About 7:30 we had breakfast, bread and honey in the comb, boiled eggs and tea. Only our party of Americans was there.

Afterwards, from our window overlooking the garden, we saw Abdul-Baha and Mirza Assadu'llah walking back and forth on the paths, sometimes stopping and conversing earnestly. I could not but think of a lion pacing in his cage, and a great sympathy and longing to serve him arose in me. Later a soldier came, carrying his gun, delivered a message and went away. An old man with a cane came to the garden gate, about fifty feet from where Abdul-Baha sat in the tent. He bowed low with his hand on his heart, talked a while at that distance and then, with deepest respect, moved backward through the gate and away.

During the days Abdul-Baha had but little time to himself. Visitors, tourists and officials came and went constantly. One afternoon came three black robed Catholic nuns, one portly woman with a black robe and no head-dress, and several ladies unveiled, with olive complexions. They were directed to the tent by the Master from his room window and he met them there later. Some of them spoke French and some English. One exclaimed: "Oh Madame, look there!" The children, Shogi, Rouhy and others were playing about the fountain and altogether it was quite a party.

THE SABBATH VISIT.

That was a Sabbath long to be remembered by us. About ten o'clock we were offered the great privilege of visiting the picture of the Manifestation, Baha'o'llah. How often has imagination tried to outline his face; how eagerly have those been questioned who had looked upon him; how earnestly has the wish been that the knowledge of him and the pilgrimage to his presence might have been made in his day.

The picture is a large photograph taken of him during the later years of his life. It is a majestic face, that of a strong, powerful, stern man, yet filled with an indescribable sweetness. Even in the photograph the majestic power shows through the lines of light and shade. I will not attempt to describe it, nor the solemnity and influence of that visit. No word was spoken. It was a time for silence. I will simply quote the writing of one who saw him in life!

"The face of him on whom I gazed I can never forget, though I cannot describe it. Those piercing eyes seemed to read one's very soul; power and authority sat on that ample brow; while the deep lines on the forehead and face implied an age which the jet-black hair and beard flowing down in indistinguishable luxuriance almost to the waist seemed to belie. No need to ask in whose presence I stood, as I bowed myself before one who is the object of a devotion and love which kings might envy and emperors sigh for in vain."*

Soon after we returned to our room Abdul-Baha came and again expressed his precious love to us, saying that he was happy that we had seen the picture. He said: "This is a blessed prison, the Holy Land, and you have seen the picture of the Blessed Perfection, and also Abdul-Baha, and we love you. You must be very glad and we are very glad. I hope the influence of this great thing will appear, and that, when you return to America, by you the Americans will be made happy. The talks I give you are like the seed which they cultivate in the ground. I hope that it will grow, and when it grows up that it will be very good."

Looking out of the window, he said: "Some of the trees in the garden have new leaves and are very beautiful, and also man, when he comes to have leaves and fruit, it is very good. Man is like the ground or earth. He is the dust,

---
*Edward G. Browne, M. A., M. B., Cambridge, England, in Introduction to "The Episode of the Bab."

and in this dust, by the bounty of God, grow up so many kinds of flowers, and from him will appear many wonderful things." He then asked one of those present what he would do when he returned to America, and then added: "It is said in the Bible that when Messiah comes he will come with many angels and with trumpets. We hope you will be that voice of the trumpet when you go to America."

LESSONS OF HUMILITY.

One forenoon Mirza Assadu'llah came to the room and talked of Abdul-Baha's teaching of decomposition, showing its great importance. Then came Mizra Hayder Ali, old and wise, beautiful, smiling, happy, a man who has suffered captivity, slavery, imprisonment and chains, everything but death, for the Cause. He talked of the spiritual embryo and its growth, its five stations and the five possessions of each religion, viz.: a prophet, a book, a law, a nation and miracles. The real birth of spiritual knowledge comes when it is perceived that these essentials pertain alike to all of the great religions, and that they all originated from the Command of God. Is it not true that in this birth lies the realization of the Fatherhood of God, the spiritual brotherhood of man, and the foundation of Universal Peace?

Those two wise old men, Mirza Hayder Ali and Mirza Assadu'llah, were like children in their happy, simple ways and evident affection. Each called the other his father, exalting the other's wisdom above his own. Mirza Hayder Ali gave each of us some sugar plums from his pocket, but overlooked Mirza Assadu'llah who sat besides him on the divan, whereupon Mirza Assadu'llah said he thought his father did not treat his son very well. Although these men have reached a maturity of knowledge far beyond our perception, yet Mirza Hayder Ali said: "Now, seeing Abdul-Baha you realize, each by himself. You see Abdul-Baha and we also see Abdul-Baha. You see and we see. As we tell you, so you must tell us also what you see. You have reached maturity as you have advanced one foot. Still we must be humble and say to others, 'Tell us.'"

He likened us to children in the Truth, just beginning to walk, and said: "In the New Testament it is related that Christ received children and said—'These are the children of the Kingdom because their hearts are pure and they speak what learned men cannot speak.' In the first degree all are as children of the Kingdom. The difference between you and us is that we came sooner than you and our faults are more, because I could not do what I ought to do during this time. I know, and I express myself, but you come newly; all Bahais are one person; *now you try to spread the Cause so that God may forgive our laziness.*"

Everywhere among the friends, at Acca,

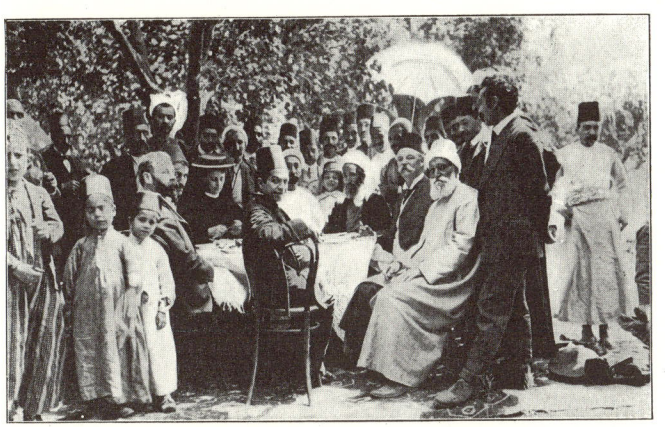

AMONG THE FRIENDS IN CAIRO

Haifa, Port Said, Alexandria and Cairo, we were given lessons of humility, simple, loving service, unselfishness and happiness in living the life of the Kingdom. There is no ostentation or striving for effect, but courtesies and offerings, a flower, a cup of tea, a bit of candy, carrying a parcel or doing some service, are blended with such a simple, affectionate spirit that they charm and attract and are in harmony with that wonderful, spiritual aura of peace and love which prevades all meetings of the friends in the Orient.

INCIDENTS.

One morning Abdul-Baha came to our room, asked how we were and how we had rested. His face was wonderfully clear and shining, fresh like water. He invited us to come into his room adjoining. It was small and plainly furnished with iron bed, table and divan. He gave each of us a photograph of the Castle of Maku in Persia where the Bab had been confined. At my request he took my large fountain pen and wrote on the back of each picture—"A gift from Abdul-Baha." Then, looking at the pen, he said: "The battle axe must fit the hand of the wielder."

Mirza Assadu'llah suggested one day that we say to Abdul-Baha that we would like to have that dinner a commemoration of the House of Spirituality; then the next day's meal in memory of the New York Council Board; and then each following day—of one of the associations or bodies of believers; then of each of the friends singly, and thus we would be enabled to stay there indefinitely, commemorating the friends. So, at dinner, he told the Master that we wished to hold that meal in commemoration of the House of Spirituality. Abdul-Baha replied—"Yes! and of all in America." Thus our scheme was completed in one day—but he went on and gave us an instruction of the unity of all, and said that as one is a representative of many in a parliament or congress, and as all are waves of one sea, so it seemed to him a reality that all the American believers were there present with him at the table. He said he would like to see the faces of them all, but that all were with him in spirit and it was not necessary that the faces should be seen.

The last day there the ladies of the household came and talked with us through an open doorway. They told us how, owing to the customs of the country, they were like caged birds, unable to fly abroad and sing the praises of God; that they could only work within the walls and beseech God with their prayers for the success and spreading of His Word throughout the world. They asked us to carry the message of their condition, their love, their hopes and prayers, to their sisters in America and ask them to so strive and work that they might accomplish not only their own duty in the Cause of God but also that of the helpless ones in the Orient.

Always there arises this idea of the oneness of mankind. If one fails to accomplish what he should do, is prevented or unable, then it becomes the duty of others to do so much more than their own duty that there may be no loss because of the lack of others. In other words, that the duty

ENTRANCE AND COURT OF THE HOUSE AT ACCA

of all is the duty of each, and that each is responsible for the results of all, just as one member of the body should do its utmost to assist and to atone for the failure of any other member. This is true vicarious atonement, arising from the innate oneness of the human race.

A HEAVENLY ATMOSPHERE.

At Acca nothing in appearance is marvelous; all is simple, direct, natural, without effort or preparation. Yet the effect is deep, strong and wonderful, because all that is said or done is an expression of complete assurance in the Truth of God, entire reliance upon His Guidance, devotion to His will and love for His service. This certainty of rightness, this abnegation of self in favor of God and His will as expressed through His Messengers and Servants, causes a simplicity and power which penetrates the hearts and kindles in them quenchless flames of love, service and unity, the triune, heavenly oneness, which shall make man at one with God, with the universe and with himself. These are the subjects of interest with Abdul-Baha. These are the matters which cause the fragrant, spiritual atmosphere, the breathing of which brings heaven on earth.

In his presence, faith in God, in the power of good, in the victory of the Spirit, became confirmed. Confidence was supreme in the impregnable certainty of the Cause of God. The

TUTOR AND PUPILS IN THE GARDEN

feeling possessed us that the Day of God's triumph was shining, that we were admitted as humble factors in his work of gladness, and that the might of man's bondage to the tyranny of self was being illumined by the Glory of God. Fear and trembling vanished; prayer and praise sang joyously within us. In his presence we realized that we were at the threshold of the Kingdom of God, and that the Spiritual fragrance of the Court of Nearness to Him poured forth through that door of selfless service to purge and purify the dense atmosphere of mankind.

THE OLD STONE STEPS

I took a picture of the old, stone steps leading to that "upper chamber." After our return to Chicago I showed it to Mr. Scheffler; he said—"Those are the steps up to heaven"—and he was right. Heaven is a condition, and it exists there. To this servant it was as if he were immersed in an acean of fragrance and peace; as if one were breathing a rich atmosphere, and drowned in a fragrant ether which penetrated through and through to the centers of beings. This atmosphere is a reality. It has been mentioned by many, and it is not an imagination, nor is it due to excitement or enthusiasm. It is a cognizable fact which enters the life and remains with him who strives to do the will of God. The presence of the Holy Spirit as a perceptible, soul-tangible actuality cannot be denied. It is there at Acca in force; it is felt by every one in some degree, even by opposers and strangers. It is a great shield of protection which defends the Cause of God forever, even though that defense may not always be in accord with the desires of the faithful. God's ways are not our ways.

The whole thought was of spiritual things, conditions and progress. The unity and brotherhood of men and peoples was the frequent consideration, always from a spiritual point of view. This talking and thinking constantly of heavenly things causes great delight. Peace, love and longing for service possessed us.

THE PALMS

CHILDREN OF THE HOUSEHOLD

Nothing visible caused that happiness within those walls; it is simply and truly the presence there of the Holy Spirit of God in overwhelming power. This sweet aroma of the Spirit radiates from that fountain of love for humanity, which pours forth so freely, so impersonally, so universally for ever soul that is wanting love. They come from every land, from every religion, from all kinds of training, each with his little cup or larger bowl, seeking answer to his quest; pilgrims from all over the world coming to that Center of the Covenant of Love, a man outwardly like themselves. And, after a week, a day, or an hour, they return to their distant homes, all *filled with love,* most of their questions unasked and forgotten, curious no longer, but satisfied and overflowing with love to the human race and a great longing to bear the Word of Revelation to their friends, and to serve every creature of God without regard to family, race or religion. The inexpressible happiness of the Spirit possesses each one of them, and he wants the whole world to have it.

THE NEW HEAVEN AND EARTH.

The most visible effect of that power is in the lives of the believers everywhere, the pilgrims from every land, and the children. Such children I have never seen, so courteous, unselfish, thoughtful for others, unobtrusive, intelligent, and swiftly self-denying in the little things that children love, such as toys, candies, fruit, etc. Wherever there were believers we found courteous, gentle, loving, earnest people, looking only for opportunities to serve one another. This effect upon the lives of all in those countries, who come in contact with this Revelation, no matter from what nation, religion or clime, proves its

CHILDREN OF THE KINGDOM

BROTHERHOOD OF MEN

universal and mighty power. And this is exactly its claim, that it is for the removal of differences and bringing the whole world into a unity of Faith, Love and Service. It is accomplishing this among all peoples, and if it shall so transform the few, it demonstrates its power, and thus it shall go on changing the hearts and lives of all who come under its influence, until all the world shall be as one great family dwelling in its heavenly—earthly home.

Herein is the oneness of mankind demonstrated—that all these varieties of men, each with different views, different methods of thought, different conceptions of religion, and opposing tendencies, after one draught at this Fountain of Instruction in the tenets of Love, fall upon each other's necks, embrace with tears of joy, and go their ways like children of one family, new born into the Kingdom of Heaven. All the differences are forgotten and are seen at their true value as of no importance compared to the great truth, the Oneness and Fatherhood of God, the oneness and brotherhood of men. Each one of them becomes a missionary of peace. The heart of each has enlarged to embrace the whole world, even his enemies; each sends his thoughts of good will and good wish to other peoples than he called his own. "His own" is forgotten in his desire for the good of the whole; yet he neglects not those near to him, for to them he can give service, and by service he must express his love.

Has such a condition as this been ever witnessed in the world before? While each nation was confined within its own boundary lines, each state a law unto itself, each religion a barbarism to all but its little circle of adherents, men could not meet together, could not know each other, and much less could they learn to love the stranger and the enemy. These conditions of acquaintance, of knowledge, of respect and of love have been made possible in this age through the wonderful inventions, the advances in means of transportation, the rapid conveyance of information, the uses of steam and electricity, and those discoveries, all of the last half century, which have leveled the mountains, raised the valleys and made the whole earth a highway for the dissemination of knowledge, wherein no "wayfarer" needs to err.

These conditions *could not be* until the coming of that "Day of God" which was promised by God's prophets age after age, "That Day" wherein the old earth and heaven should pass away like a scroll that is read and finished, and a new earth should be created in order that a new heaven should be also created thereon. How blind is he who cannot see the hand of more than man in all these wonders.

THE SERVANT OF GOD.

Abdul-Baha is a grand man, broad, universal in thought, standing above the world and looking down upon it in its weakness and poverty with a boundless love and an intense longing to lift it up from its wretchedness, to make it conscious of the rich bounties of God, which are so freely offered in this wonderful time, to remove the differences to bring all men, all peoples, all religions into true manhood and religion, for in reality there is but one manhood and one religion. He stands there erect, with extended arms, the Master of the Feast, calling with a loud, clear voice to all mankind: "Come! Come! Come! Now is the time! Now is the accepted time! Come and drink of this sweet Water which is pouring in torrents upon all parts of the world!"

And, as each hungry pilgrim comes to that prison house, that banquet hall of heavenly gifts, he takes him in his arms and draws him to his breast with such sincerity and enthusiasm of love that the petty cares, thoughts and ambitions of the world vanish away, and one is at peace and in happiness because he has reached home and found love there. Father, mother, brother, all are welcoming, greeting and embracing the wanderer in that simple, natural welcome of Abdul-Baha. One wishes that the embrace might not end, it is so joyful, so comforting. Truly, I think it never does end. It opens a door of love which shall never be closed. *The home of the heart is there.*

It is the home of the universal love, not that of the individual alone. He is no respecter of persons. His own personality in the eyes of others is naught to him, nor does he care for the personality of others. It is not love for the individual one, but the Love of the Spirit for humanity. Each visitor is only one of the waves of that great ocean of mankind, and is a type, a representative of the whole. When the Servant of God embraces one, He embraces all in that one.

THE LAW OF LOVE.

This law of love was wonderfully proved when the Persian, Jewish and Zoroastrian pilgrims came to visit us, one, two and three at a time, many of them, and also two old friends who had been with Baha'o'llah in Baghdad in the early days of trial, and Mirza Esmu'llah, a sweet old man and learned teacher. All showed the same beautiful spirit of affection and happiness. Although we were from widely separated religions, countries and races, yet we sobbed with joy as we were clasped in each other's arms. It seemed as if the millenium had actually arrived, that mankind had lost all differences, that Love had conquered the world, and that we were standing within the threshold of heaven and in the presence of God. Abdul-Baha was not personally present at those meetings, but the Spirit of God, the Spirit of Love, the Spirit of Peace, was there. The tears of those lovers of God flowed with gladness, their eyes shone, their faces beamed, their courtesy was unsurpassed, their sincerity manifest, their devotion to the Cause of God supreme. They clearly see in such meetings of pilgrims from different lands the beginning of fulfillment of the prophesies relating to the spreading over the whole world of the knowledge of the One God, Creator and Father of all. This coming together of representatives of several religions in loving embrace with tears of joy is a certain and marvelous proof of the truth and power of this Bahai Revelation.

All bowed when they entered the room after removing their shoes, and placed their hands on their hearts and foreheads, exclaiming—"Alhamdu Lellah!" (Praise be to God!) and other words of thankfulness. Then they opened their arms for embraces and expressions of love. None sat until requested, and not then until the host was seated. After talking for a while through interpreters, they again embraced and bade us an affectionate and ardent farewell, and went backward with deep respect to the door where they put on their shoes. It should be noted that this meeting was an event of a lifetime; that in Persia they had been told that there were no American Bahai believers, that the tales of them were false, and, when they actually met four such believers, three men and one woman, there in the house of Abdul-Baha, their gladness overflowed in most sincere expressions of affection and unity.

Mirza Esmu'llah spoke of the rapid spread of of the Cause, beyond his hope or expectation, and of the wonderful inventions since the advent of Baha'o'llah, all due to the breeze of the Holy Spirit, which was blowing and bringing the Springtime of the New Day to the world. A bright, intelligent, young Jew from Hamadan, Persia, said that at the request of his parents he had just visited old Jerusalem during Holy Week, and from there he went to Bethlehem where he "sat down and wept" for the things his people had done to Messiah in the old days. This was the effect upon him of the Bahai teachings concerning Jesus. He was asked what he found at Jerusalem. He replied: "The city was there, but the owner was gone. I came to Acca and found the owner of the city here." He said that in Hamadan were over six hundred Jew-Bahais who were known, and there were others not known openly.

The millenium in very truth was in those gatherings. It has arrived. It has drawn the people of the earth together in the bonds of love to God and love to man. The differences between peoples and religions have not been argued away, not changed by debate, not removed by law nor by war, but they have been *dissolved in the fires of love,* and have disappeared like mists before the morning sun of Godly knowledge. "Not by might, nor by power, but by my Spirit, saith the Lord of hosts." When man rises above those differences in the atmosphere of Spiritual Truth, his humanity, his sympathy, his human affection, spring forth and blossom in the land of the spirit, so that greed and ambitions are forgotten, and only love remains. This is the elixir of Unity; this is the solvent that shall melt the hearts of men and bring that "Most Great Peace," which Baha'o'llah said "must come." When the spirits of men actually come into contact with the Spirit of this Day, this greatest Revelation from God, this spirit of self-abnegating service to mankind, they simply melt and unite, and all other matters and things pass into the realm of the unimportant.

UNITY, LOVE AND SERVICE.

A great lesson impressed upon us at Acca was the waste of time and strength in observing and struggling with the *little things,* the annoyances, the actions or efforts of opposers, the disagreeables which crowd against us in life. Rather should we look only at the good, strengthen and encourage the good, sure in confidence that the worthless will fade away and that it is powerless against the valuable. To look at things in a larger way than some of us have done; to take our point of view from the mountain of the Holy Spirit, and, with full reliance thereon, to devote ourselves to those things which are its servants. Resolved into daily life, this means to overcome evil with good, to heed not personal desires and ambitions, but rather endeavor to serve others, make our lives useful, to serve the good in others and veil the evil in them; to judge not, but, looking keenly for the good, to encourage that good by wise and loving service.

Service is the key to unity, and Unity is the one great theme of the Teacher of Acca. Without unity nothing can be accomplished. As the unity of the world is the aim and purpose of this Bahai Revelation, that unity must begin at home; unity of the few, the assembly, many assemblies, the country, many countries, the world. As the family is the symbol of the home and its peaceful unity, so must the Bahai assemblage be the type and foundation of the whole. And unity which is confined to the society or assembly alone is *not unity;* it must be open armed unity, seeking oneness of will, of purpose and of work with all other groups and assemblies. Each individual strengthens his individuality, not by maintaining it alone, but, on the contrary, by joining himself, his powers and abilities with others. Thus his own efficiency is enlarged and multiplied by cohesion with others. As a single letter is of small worth compared to its value in a word and greater value in a sentence, so the individual man must enter into combination with all that he possibly can for the strengthening of the Cause of God and humanity, and this means the increased worth of himself.

This in reality is the Message of Baha'o'llah in this Day—Unity, Love and Service in the Name of God; service in love, service to the friends and to all; living with such sweetness, usefulness, happiness and cheerfulness that the life of itself attracts the notice of others and draws them to the beauty of such living; service to every one around, no discrimination in service, but simply a great desire to be of use in every possible waking moment to some one of God's creatures.

Some money was offered to Abdul-Baha. He took the gold in his hand, held it for a moment and then passed it back, saying: "Give this to the poor, the very, very poor. *Do not discriminate in favor of any one sect or people, but give to all.*" His instruction concerning that money is the teaching for our lives. The poorer, the more needy, more helpless, more ignorant, the more bitter or hateful one is, the more shall we serve that one with goodness, sweetness, patience, forbearance, helpfulness and love. This is the teaching to-day of Baha'o'llah and of his blessed Son.

Every instruction of Abdul-Baha is of value for *living*. His simple words are, as he says, seeds which, if they be sown in the heart and cultivated there, grow into beautiful trees of knowledge and wisdom. As one ponders, they develop new meanings and inner significances which are pregnant with power; and they are all thoroughly practical in their application to life. He ascribes everything to the "Power of the Word of God," and his only desire is that God's Will and God's Word may spread and conquer the hearts of men.

THE FEAST OF FELLOWSHIP.

The last evening before we left Acca, Abdul-Baha asked us to meet all the friends at supper and to speak to them as Mr. MacNutt and Mr. Harris had done when there. About forty gathered in the large upper balcony room at nine o'clock. Abdul-Baha excused himself from visitors in the tent and came to us. He took a napkin from a plate at the table and handing it to one, said: "Bia inja" (Come here). Then he gave a napkin to another, and so on to all, placing each guest where he desired him to be. It was a beautiful example of hostship and personal attention.

When all were seated he walked up and down and around the long table, teaching us of the bounty of God and its victory over the hearts of men—words of heavenly encouragement—after which he withdrew to his visitors awaiting him in the tent. His words were as follows:

"It is a good gathering. Thank God that believers are gathered around this table from every part with utmost sincerity, unity and friendship. I beg of God that, as we are gathered in this contingent world around this table, we may also be gathered in the world of the Kingdom and be united. I hope that the gathering together of the believers may be the source of unity and harmony of all the people of the world; that this physical table may be a symbol of the heavenly table.

"Christ said that he was the heavenly bread which was sent down from heaven, and this bread means the heavenly table. I hope tonight that heavenly blessings may descend upon you; that you may be born again, a new spirit, a new power, a new life. God's abundances and favors are boundless, without end, and the blessings of Baha'o'llah are like a boundless ocean. One wave of the ocean of his blessings will cover (drown) all the mountains of the world. Now these waves are rolling upon your heads. I hope you will be drowned in these waves. You will get endless, boundless blessings and bounties.

"This material world is very dark, and this handful of dust is very narrow. I hope that the doors of divine worlds may be opened before your faces; that you may soar up in a space whose

light is eternal; enter a garden whose fruits are everlasting; become the center of human virtues and the appearances of divine perfections; your hearts be adorned with the commemoration of God; your faces illumined with the light of the love of God; that your ears may hear the melodies of sanctity; your spirits may be gladdened with divine glad-tidings; your tongues may move in praising God; in short, that you may attain to such a station as to be called the children of the Kingdom."

The courses served were of delicious foods, ending with sweet confections and oranges. The Persian pilgrims, ten or more, were on the left of the long table, wearing red fezzes. Aged men with white fezzes, green and white turbans, flowing robes, full beards, faces of dignity, sweetness and rare intelligence, bordered the table. Many of them were old believers who had passed through the fires of persecution and several were closely related to some of the martyrs. A finer, more dignified or as notable an assemblage would be hard to find. Some of their names will be remembered when those of kings are forgotten. There were children also at the table, but only one woman, Mrs. Agnew, although the ladies of the household were doubtless present, seeing and hearing though not in sight.

After the meal Mr. Agnew, Mr. Scheffler and this servant spoke as requested. The utmost attention was paid by all, even those "grave and reverend seniors" before whom we were as little children in knowledge. Then, sweet old Mirza Hayder Ali came near the head of the table, and, sitting next to Mirza Assadu'llah, talked wisely and pleasantly for a few moments. Then all arose, embraced each other and us, and retired to their quarters.

THE WORLD'S MATURITY.

There are no apparent miracles at Acca, but the great miracle is the spreading of the Word and the knowledge of the Bahai Revelation over the world from that prison spot, that apparently helpless source, during the last fifteen years. It is marvelous. It appears everywhere. It is being accepted by advancing souls of every race and religion. It is attracting attention from journals and magazines of many countries, Russia, India, Persia, France, England and America. All the powers of nature are working with it. Abdul-Baha said: *"Hitherto the world has been as a child at the breast, able to receive and manifest but little of the powers of the Spirit. Now it is entering the age of its maturity, and it is possible for the divine teachings, confirmations, bounties and Spiritual Laws of God to appear perfectly because now there is capacity.*

In olden times it was said by God that the sign of the true prophet should be that what he said should come to pass. Truly this is the sign of to-day. The words of the Blessed Perfection, Baha'o'llah, and those of Abdul-Baha penetrate the hearts of men to the core. They do not return void to Him who sent them forth. They affect the lives; they uplift the souls; they give new birth to the spirits of men; they draw all together in the One Name of God; they cause Godly characteristics to take the place of animal qualities; they bring love, peace, union, harmony, service, happiness and joy in place of hatred, strife, oppression and greed.

The words uttered within those prison walls have gone forth through all the world carrying the gifts of God to the hearts of men. Are these things of God? Can an evil tree bear such fruit? Can the helpless, the powerless, the prisoners, the despised, the oppressed, manifest such power, such strength, such victories, save by the might of the All-Glorious One? Praise be to His Holy Name!

Moreover, the world in every part, in each plane of life, in science, art, invention, discovery, in thought and ideal, in word and deed, is carrying out daily with increasing and rapid growth the very conditions that the Blessed Messenger of God declared should be. Was this a Prophet, a Man of God? One needs but to take His Words, the "Hidden Words" and *live them;* he will know for himself, "and not by the knowledge of another." He that *doeth the works shall* know whether they be of God.

THE PARTING.

In the forenoon of the last day Abdul-Baha called each one of us separately to his reception room for a private interview and definite instruction. He said he wished for us to remain longer, but, on account of threatening troubles, it was better that we should go. Certain messages and communications were given to him by us, which he took and marked for later consideration. He bade us carry his message of love and happiness to the friends, and urged the utmost importance of unity and harmony of all believers. With such unity the Cause of God would prosper and spread rapidly; without it there could be no progress. He hoped that he should hear of our work in America. At the last meal he spoke of the building of the Temple in this country and said it was of very great importance, and should become a means of blessed association and unity among the friends.

I did not say good-bye. Soon after the noon meal Abdul-Baha met me in the little upper court. He embraced this servant, and, moving away a few feet, he turned, looked steadily and pronounced a promise that is a precious memory and hope. Then he went into the apartments of the household. A little later we were called to go. We descended the old, stone stairway, with friends watching us from the grated windows, crossed the lower court, passed through the archway and out to the carriage awaiting us.

AQUEDUCT BESIDE THE ROAD TO THE TOMB

As we entered the world again it was with a sort of chill as when one steps from a warm room into a cold night air. Curious eyes watched us as we rode again through the city, the cramped streets and crooked ways, to the outer gate where we waited for the third horse of the team. There we were surrounded by vendors and beggers calling out the names of the loved one we had left, evidently hoping thus to extract money from us. We had descended from a realm of happiness, peace and light to an underworld of greed and strife. Never before had we so perceived the ignorance and animalism which possesses men, and at first we shrank from them, but when we noted their condition, their sickness, their burdens and griefs, a longing tenderness welled up in our hearts toward them and to all creatures, a great wish to pour out on them the fragrances of peace, good-will and love, to lift them up from darkness to light, from ignorance to knowledge, from hell to heaven—and to serve them, even to the extinction of self. The contrast between the

THE SPREADING MULBERRY TREES

world and that "Prison" we had left was so strong that it intensified the consciousness of that heavenly condition in which we had dwelt during those blessed days and nights.

THE TOMB AND THE RIZWAN.

When we had left the city, Mirza Moneer, the faithful interpreter, joined us, and we drove two miles to the Garden of Behje and visited the Tomb of Baha'o'llah. There we removed our shoes and entered that consecrated place with melting hearts. In the large, outer room or court were beautiful rugs, vases and flowers, and a central garden railed around. A little breeze came through the open windows and caused the many glass prisms, pendent from lamps and chandeliers, to jangle sweetly together. It was

OVER LAND AND WATER

a soft chiming in the silence, fitting and beautiful. Each one alone entered the inner chamber of the tomb, and remained as long as possible, communing with God and remembering the friends far away before the Presence which unmistakably was there. Again we were constrained to silence, for each soul was occupied with his God. It was the culmination of our pilgrimage.

From there we drove a short distance to the Garden of the Rizwan, met the old gardener, Mirza Abul Kasim, took tea with him under the spreading mulberry trees (the "tent without poles or covering"), and rested by the seat which was "over land and water" where the Great Manifestation used to sit. We saw his plain room in the house at the end of the garden, and noted how tenderly everything was preserved and cared for. We sympathized with Mirza Abul Kasim in his pride and love for that Garden of his Lord. The thoughts and emotions of years were crowded for us into that one day. We were overwhelmed with love, praise and thankfulness. Through all the nine mile drive to Haifa we scarcely spoke, for words disturbed the oceans in our souls. Like tired and happy children we went again to the "Hospice of the Little Child."

On my return to America I found the friends eager to hear my impressions of Acca and especially of Abdul-Baha, and I have tried to tell somewhat of them in this and other writings; but the certain, clear and correct expression of him

IN THE GARDEN OF THE RIZWAN

is that which he declares in his own words, viz.: that he is Abdul-Baha, the Servant of Glory—that is, the Servant of God; that he has no station, no purpose, no claim, no wish, no existence except that of Abdul-Baha. He asks most earnestly that no one shall ascribe to him any mission or station other than that of the Servant of God. Those who really desire to obey his will and comply with his wish, rather than to uphold their own imaginations, will do literally as he has requested.

In truth, no title can be nobler than this; no glory is greater than service; no station higher than that of sacrifice; no honor greater than to be the instrument of the Spirit. He who serves God is truly in the image of God, and he who sacrifices himself for love of man is the Exemplar of the Love of God. It is enough that Abdul-Baha is the Example and Leader of all mankind in service, sacrifice, love and peace, fulfilling before all the Law of the Kingdom as declared by the Great Manifestation, Baha'o'llah.

IN WONDERLAND

In Wonderland

We lived in wonderland at Acca. Had we been children visiting in some royal palace, with furnishings richer than our expectations or beyond even our imaginations, the wonder would not have been greater. While in reality we were living in a prison and for a week we had not left our room except to go into the dining room adjoining or into the little walled-in court scarcely larger than our room—all on the upper story.

Our room was clean and neat but very plain and simple. There was a straw matting over the stone floor and over this in the center under the little table was thrown a Persian rug. On either side of the room was a single iron bedstead and along the end of the room was a low divan covered with white muslin. In one corner on the plain, board walls were some hooks for hanging clothes and in the other stood an iron wash stand with towels. The center table held, each day, a fresh and beautiful bouquet of flowers and at night a lamp was lit and placed upon it.

The walls, the floor, the stairs were stone, worn by age and chipped and broken by the elements.

Such were the physical surroundings, yet when we left, the commonplace things of the world seemed strange to us; it seemed as if we had left our home and were going out into a strange country, and yet withal a feeling of security and peace possessed us. We wished to be silent. It was an inner consciousness. And of this wonder we were not entirely outwardly aware until we noted in each other's eyes the dreamy look of preoccupation, to be suddenly aroused to find that we in thought were back in Acca, to find that some great change had taken place within us, that we had been living in a land of spiritual wonder, that our souls were astonished at the power of the spirit of God. And in this wonderland our souls expanded and a great realization and longing for the things of God possessed us. As a tulip, wet with dew, opens its cup in the glory of the sunbeam, so our souls were opened in that fragrant atmosphere of spirit to an understanding of the power and love of God.

In that love our souls were bathed, refreshed, enkindled. It was sweet, fragrant, charming, delightful. These are only words, but if it is charming, it is charming; if it is delightful, how can it be more so? Yet these are mere words used to describe that ecstatic state when human spirit meets the spirit of Love Divine tuned to its comprehension, words used to describe that which must forever remain indescribable—the realization in our hearts of the surrounding presence of Divine Faith and Love.

When one enters the peace of that glorious home all the world is left outside. Through all the friends at Acca, and there are some forty persons in that household, there flows the happy, joyous, fragrant spirit of love. It seems in all of them without distinction and creates an atmosphere powerful in the extreme. It is an evidence of the Spirit's power. "Not by might, nor by power, but by my Spirit." It is a forecast of what the whole world shall be.

But while it seems in all of these dear souls without distinction, it really is in them only by reflection of the spirit in Abdul-Baha. The burden of it all devolves on him. In him is the decision, the responsibility; he is the center, all others reflect the spirit which they find in him.

And he tells us he is the servant and reflector of the spirit of Baha'o'llah, that it was in Him the Great Light shown: Baha'o'llah, the Great Manifestation! And I knew this to be true.

We looked upon the photograph of Baha'o'llah. It is the face of one in whom the human spirit had been "driven to the wall;" the face of one who had "found his beloved in the garden" of his heart; in whom a wondrous power was evident, not to oppose but to submit, and submitting to conquer the opposers. There can be no doubt of the source of that wondrous power which sits upon that brow as on a throne of majesty, which rises up, unbidden as a maiden's blush, upon that face with rarest beauty. It is the Blessed Beauty, the Blessed Perfection. It is the face of him in whom no wish nor desire is found save the will of God. It is the Face of God—the lights of all the attributes of God play over it.

Whatever may be the reasoning of my mind regarding this most profound experience of my life, however I may explain it to myself, seeking to give a reason for the faith within me, and however foolish it may seem to others, the fact remains that in a moment—with feelings of awe and reverence and realizations of the majesty and greatness of that Face of God—I bowed myself prostrate upon the floor and laid my spirit, soul and self upon the altar of His Love. Something in that Face demanded of me obedience and something in my heart obeyed with joy and gladness.

When next we looked upon the face of Abdul-Baha, we saw therein reflected the light of knowledge and of power which made the face of Baha'o'llah so beautiful. I realize now, that ere my mind gave up itself and bowed before the majecty of Baha'o'llah in that moment it recognized in the lines of face and brow the evidence of majesty, power and knowledge—not such as when the tyrant of the human will spurs on the jaded brain to search for thoughts and flounder in expression—but welling up, as from a spring eternal, the Holy Spirit flows in joy and gladness, in holiness and glory, a never ending flood of knowledge, light and love for all mankind.

And now in unity with the Holy Spirit which manifested in Baha'o'llah stands Abdul-Baha, the Branch, through whom flows the same life-giving Spirit to build this great edifice of love in the hearts of men.

And how we knew this I cannot tell. I cannot analyze it. The Holy Spirit is above the grasp of man. It lifts man up to its own height of realization and perception of truth, establishing in him Its confirmation and assurance but It does not allow man to draw It down to his limitation, that he may express It in his words, or confine It in a creed or dogma.

One evening Abdul-Baha came into the room to answer our questions. We wrote down the answers beside the questions which friends had given us to ask, in the note book kept for that purpose. His words were full of advice and exhortation. When this was finished, he said: "Now lay aside your note book and let us visit together." He sat upon the divan, asked me to sit beside him, placed his arm around my shoulders (as a father would a child), laid my head over against his forehead and opened his lips in words of love and encouragement. He spoke freely with great power and feeling. There was no barrier between him and me save the barrier of my own limitation. The ocean of love was flowing, the cup of my heart was full and could take no more. This was the only barrier between him and me. I could not touch him, though his hand lay lovingly upon my shoulder. I had nothing to offer, but he offered the fellowship of the Kingdom—offered it all, everything, freely—I might take so much as I was able. He would have exchanged places with me, but I was not able, I had not the capacity—over me rolled great billows of love—enough for all humanity.

But that evening the eye of my soul saw another vision and a glimpse into another world whose power is unequalled, which accomplishes its purpose without warfare or strife, without causing unhappiness or destruction, which is above opposition, to which the intellect cannot reach, which loses nothing of its attraction because it is the same for all, one atom of which is sufficient for all creatures while the rolling ocean of its power envelops all humanity and must accomplish the end for which He hath ordained it. It is the Love of God.

In that atmosphere the One who created me laid His loving hand upon the heartstrings, struck the inner chord of my being and within my soul the song must sing. It is the song of the redeemer, the song the sower sings as he goes forth to sow, and the song the reaper sings when he gathers in the golden grain. It is the song of existence, the song of life, the song of joy, the song of triumph.

I realize my utter lack of power to express in words this wonderful spirit. I have tried it with some of my most intimate, close and sympathetic friends and have not been able to carry its message, and to my own self I must admit my failure for when I attempt to describe this wonderful spirit, my words do not describe it to myself. I can only find the expression of this spirit in the words of Baha'o'llah and Abdul-Baha. This glorious attainment God has reserved for His messengers that they may lay their hearts open before the world, that through the conquering power of self-surrender the living sacrifice may overcome the world, and men come to know of unity and love.

At times when reading the Book of Ighan (Certainty) the spirit of light, joy and gladness has come over me, which I have not been able to ascribe to any word or sentence or to any one idea or thought. It has seemed like a radiance arising from the Book, from the Certainty of Truth.

We lived continually in this radiant atmosphere at Acca. Did it arise from a perception of the Certainty of Truth above the operation of the mind to follow? The subtle spirit of Love Divine, all love excelling, in which we lived at Acca, to which the depth of our natures responded and called it the Love and Presence of God, this spirit is in the words of Baha'o'llah and Abdul-Baha, finds expression therein, can be taken from them by the pure in heart, is creative of all the high qualities and powers of perfect living and pure thinking, creates within the heart a tenderness and power to love, to serve, to sympathize, to help, to forget the self, to grow more charitable, more kind, more willing servants, to surrender our own human will in the dawning consciousness of the knowledge of the will of God; gives us knowledge and the strength to do His will, gives us the idea and the power to execute it.

The very atmosphere of Acca, within that home made holy by the presence of Baha'o'llah, is charged with a wonderful spirit. All things there are affected by it. It enters into every action and every word.

Words which emanate from that White Spot are charged with the Holy Spirit. The Word of God has always been the same. The inner-significance, the great reality deposited in the words from the lips of the Prophets and Manifestations of God has always been the same reality, whether in Abraham, Moses, Jesus, Mohammed, the Bab, or Baha'o'llah; but now, It has come for the establishment of the Kingdom, to bring love and unity among mankind. The power of the sunlight is always the same, though in the spring it brings out the delicate blossoms and in the autumn it produces the bountiful harvest.

And now it is the "harvest time" and the seeds sown in all the previous dispensations are bearing fruit. The words of Jesus through the spread of the Gospel have proclaimed unto every nation the coming of the Kingdom, as a witness unto them; and now, from that prison town of Acca, in the shelter of the Holy Mount Carmel trodden by the feet of all the Prophets, is going forth today a living message laden with a Wonderful Spirit, proclaiming the Kingdom, taking away the barriers from the hearts of men, that all mankind may live together as one family in unity and love.

I cannot say that my ideals were realized in the Holy Presence in that White Spot; in truth, it was quite different from my anticipation. The first meeting with Abdul-Baha was like being shaken severely and made to stand up squarely upon my feet; shaken, that is from my preconceived ideas and stood up squarely to lift my head into the sunlight of the Truth of God and take a deep breath of the true atmosphere of the Spirit of God. We met not our ideals but the will of God. His ideas are not our ideas. It is well when we can set aside the ideals born of our own imagination, limited to our imperfect grasp of Truth and take for our own the ideals set before us by one who has the perfect knowledge with which God endows His Manifestation. May all the sincere and earnest people of the world come into oneness of ideal in unity with Abdul-Baha, the Center of the Covenant, as he is in unity and oneness of ideal with Baha'o'llah, the Manifestation of God.

It is not possible for everyone to make the visit to Acca. Were it possible Abdul-Baha wishes he might meet every loving soul in the world. But everyone may meet the Spirit enclosed within the words; and we met not a man in Acca but the Holy Spirit radiant, vibrant in a man, and those who cannot make the visit may find the Holy Spirit radiant, vibrant in the words "concealed within the tents" of His utterance; and those who have sought and found therein the "pearl of greatest price," who have found the "treasure hidden in the field" will not exchange it for all the world.